HOW TO

FISH GOOD

"Pardon me, Miss," he spoke in his resonant voice, "but see what I caught on my wet fly, up on Maggie's Riffle!"

"Indeed!" replied the winsome lass to the husky stranger. "And that's a most attractive mini-fig you're wearing!"

(**Chapter Lxxvii**, "The Use of Apples as Bait.")

HOW TO

FISH GOOD

(Fearless Facts about Lying, Cheating,
Thieving, Poaching & other Ancient
and Honorable Piscatorial Practices)

Written, punctuated & illustrated

by

Milford ("Stanley") Poltroon

WINCHESTER PRESS

Library of Congress Catalog Card Number: 78-163779
ISBN: 0-87691-051-7

Published by Winchester Press,
460 Park Avenue, New York 10022
PRINTED IN THE UNITED STATES OF AMERICA

Piscatorial Preface

In the past 87 years, 17,893 books on fishing have been published, dealing with everything from fly-tying to sex habits of the foulmouth bass. Yet amazingly enough, no one until now has written a simple straightforward treatise on *How To Fish Good!* This is the major reason why, apart from myself and 3 of my friends, there are no good fishermen.

A lesser reason is that but few fishermen know how to read. That is why this book has so many beautiful pictures.

MILFORD ("STANLEY") POLTROON

DEDICATION

Dedications in most books usually say something like

"TO HORTENSE,
FLORA AND TRIXIE,
without whom this Work
would not have been possible."

Bullfrog! This dandy book would have been possible without *anybody* except the swell, lovable author. In fact, if it hadn't been for people getting in the way and knocking things over, it would have been finished lots sooner. Even so, Milford ("Stanley") Poltroon grudgingly admits the following folk did have something or other to do with it:

NOAH WEBSTER, who determined how each & every word in this well-spelled book should be properly constructed.

SALLY RILEY is not only Postmaster at West Yellowstone, Montana (there are no Mistresses in the Postal Dep't., so far as is known), but also helped pioneer the proper packaging for mailing a moose. Sally made available, at normal list price, the postage stamps without which the mss. for this inspiring book would not have reached the publisher.

IRVING ROYAL, inventor of the gas-powered typewriter on which the manuscript for this memorable work was typed.

6

BIG GEORGE, arch-enemy of conservation, who chopped down all the trees necessary to make the paper on which this collector's-item-book is printed. ➡

AL POLTROON is a shining inspiration to the Youth of our Country, having been born with two physical handicaps. He managed to overcome his stuttering and has learned how to live with the other one. Al is not only Litter & Pollution Editor of the *Wretched Mess News,* but helped with the ink placement on some of the pictures in this well-illustrated book.

HIGGINS BLACK, creator of the ink with which the illustrations for this heart-warming work were rendered (all unsuitable for framing). ➡

BILLY GRAHAMCRACKER is Religion and Bingo Editor of the *Wretched Mess News.* His tastefully run blackjack games in West Yellowstone provided funds for peanut butter, paper clips and other adhesives, with which pages of this 100% organic book were held together.

LYDIA SHELTERDOVE, the all-powerful secret Boss of the *Wretched Mess* Empire, who managed to type the entire manuscript for this unforgettable work, despite a delicate stomach condition.

DEDICATION (Continued)

CAL DUNBAR, West Yellowstone's Friendly Neighborhood Grocer, whose always-fresh baloney served as inspiration for this uplifting work.

ROBERTA POLTROON, Garbage & Cooking Editor of the *Wretched Mess News*, who faithfully stood ready to leap into action if the publisher had rejected this fat-free work.

COLONEL P. S. DEEMS, Foreign Correspondent Overseas for the *Wretched Mess News*, who thoughtfully agreed not to translate this multi-page book into French.

WINCHESTER PRESS, who possessed the raw courage necessary to publish this hitherto-unpublished work.

JANE FONDA, who generously refrained from conducting any protest demonstrations against this book.

STANLEY P. DOG, the author's ever-faithful pedigreed Fenwick Fish Retriever, who kept Forces of Evil at bay while this Pulitzer-prize-candidate work was being composed.

This Book is especially dedicated to HARRIET BEECHER POLTROON, whom we see here sharing, with the author, an epicurean extravaganza of boiled bones and Gallo Thunderbird '70 (a great year). Harriet Beecher serves as Sex & Garden Editor of the *Wretched Mess News,* albeit in a severe northerly climate such as West Yellowstone offers, there are but a scant 3 months out of the entire year when any gardening is possible. Harriet Beecher's fragrant blooming hibiscus served to counterpoint the aromatic fish which the author frequently brought home, for inspiration, while writing this classic work.

For curious reasons, Ed Zern, who wrote the FOREWORD on the facing page, has never allowed his picture to be taken.* The man shown above is not Zern, but President Theodore Roosevelt with his pet muskie, "Ed."

* See "Evil Spirits Lurk in Cameras," p. 86.

How To Write Forewords Good, or Fair

When I first met him at a large trap shoot, or "gang bang," Milford Poltroon was palming himself off as someone named "Bascom" (a word he invented, just as the Russians invented "Comintern" and Lenny Bruce invented "mother"; it is derived from "basically commercial," as he was then in the advertising business). Poltroon, or "Bascom," had an advertising agency in San Francisco, where he wrote funny ads about peanut butter and became known throughout the advertising world as the peanut butter copywriter's peanut butter copywriter, or "Max" for short.

Now, peanut butter, whatever else you may say about it, is not especially side-splitting, at least compared to fishermen. Most people can sit and look at a jar of peanut butter for days on end without so much as cracking a smile. But show me someone who can sit and look at a fisherman for more than, oh, say three or four minutes without breaking into veritable gales of laughter and I will show you someone who can sit and look at a fisherman for more than, oh, say three or four minutes without breaking into veritable gales of laughter, or has a cracked lip, or is astigmatic. Not only that, but fishermen rarely stick to the roof of your mouth, which proves that there is some good in all of us.

So when Poltroon quit the advertising business and started a magazine called *The Wretched Mess News* (a name he was forced to use, since the names *Women's Wear Daily* and *Floor Coverings Review*, his first choices, had already been taken) and began writing funny stuff about fishermen, it came out even funnier than the stuff he had been writing about peanut butter. Connoisseurs of humor began collecting old copies of *Wretched Mess News* and turning them in at Boy Scout drives for recycling.

Now, fearful that some of Poltroon's fishumor might not survive, Winchester Press has gone and put out this book at considerable trouble and expense, and it seems to me the least you can do is buy it and read it, or at least look at the pictures, for many of which Poltroon posed stark naked.

Of course if you have only a limited budget for this sort of thing and would prefer to wait until *my* book of funny stuff about fishing* comes out, why, after all it's your money.

ED ZERN

**A Fine Kettle of Fish Stories,* by Ed Zern; Winchester Press, 1972

The 5 Cardinal Principles
of Successfully Fishing Good

1. REMOVE ALL CLOTHING.   (See photograph above.) Your common sense tells you that a fish is suspicious of anything unnatural or foreign to its environment. Clothing does not occur naturally in trout streams. Fishing is difficult enough without placing unnecessary obstacles in your way. *Take it all off*.

2. PROTEIN ALONE ISN'T ENOUGH.   When you're busy fishing, your body craves energy. So don't be afraid of fats and sugars. Your system converts alcohol into rich body sugars. Remember that.

3. EXACT CHANGE.   Busses and, where they still exist, trolley cars often play an important role. Failure to have the exact change may cause a needless delay that can prove costly.

4. DON'T BE A SHOW-OFF.   Some people apparently feel compelled to periodically change their styles of dress and dancing. The fish in our wilderness streams, however, are no different from what they were when "civilized" man first saw them. So don't go around trying to impress your tastes and behavior patterns on others.

5. NO SPITTING.   Remember, a fish considers the stream or lake his home. How would you like it if someone came into YOUR home uninvited and started spitting all over your living room rug?

By keeping his portable bowl full of chicken noodle soup, *Wretched Mess News'* staff psychiatrist Wetley P. Bedford is able to forecast weather with remarkable accuracy. When the soup emits steam clouds, hot weather is close at hand. When it becomes frozen solid, this tells Bedford that a cold front is approaching.

HOW TO

FORECAST
WEATHER

GOOD

A hallmark of a good fisherman is his ability to forecast weather, and make preparations accordingly. If it is going to rain, for example, the prudent angler stops by his nearest drygoods store and purchases a raincoat, or he goes into the saloon next door and waits until it all blows over.

The first step in accurate weather forecasting is a rudimentary knowledge of clouds. All clouds divide into 4 basic types:

1. Cumulus   3. Cirrus
2. Stratus   4. Big old bastards

The latter are the only ones to worry about, since they are hollow and have their insides completely filled with rain. They can be readily identified by their size (big), and soggy appearance. The characteristic lumps all over their exterior come about as a consequence of all that water sloshing and whooshing around their insides.

If one of these clouds gets punctured, it is certain to rain. The things to watch out for are ducks, geese, airplanes, Frisbees and other flying objects that can penetrate such clouds and start them leaking. Prior to the invention of airplanes and zeppelins, rainfall in the U.S.A. was considerably less than it is today.

The prudent fisherman always wears a soft cotton cap of good quality. When the cap becomes soaking wet, this is nature's way of telling him that it is raining, or that he fell in. In either case, he takes prompt action.

Such a cap is useful in other ways, too. If, for example, it goes sailing through the air for fifty yards or more with no visible help, this tells the experienced woodsman that a strong wind is blowing. And if it suddenly bursts into flame, Mother Nature is saying that he is in the midst of a raging forest fire.

HOW TO
CHOOSE
YOUR
EQUIPMENT
GOOD

Your principal piece of fishgear is your fishing pole, or rod. People often ask me, "What's the difference between a fish pole and a rod?" "$33.75," I tell them. I seldom have time to loiter about and give them the more detailed reply, which is as follows:

A fish *pole* is any old stick of wood. It can be a length of bamboo, a piece of willow that you cut right at streamside or even an old mop handle. Most fisherfolk make their own pole, but some hardware stores and bait shops, especially in the South, sell them. A top quality fish pole will cost you as much as 87¢, but there's no need to go this high for a good beginner's outfit.

You simply tie a length of good-quality string or twine to the end of your fish pole, affix a hook suitable for the impalement of nightcrawlers or grasshoppers on the yonder end of the line, and there you are. The reel, a relatively recent affectation of anglers anyway, is dispensed with altogether.

The fishing *rod* is a jointy thing made by Fenwick or Scientific Anglers or Shakespeare or one of those other fancypants outfits that run flashy ads in *Outdoor Sports Afield & Stream,* showing some tomfool holding up a dead fish that he purportedly caught with the help of the advertised fishing rod, *or so they would have you believe.*

You can pay $350 and more for a custom split bamboo fishing rod. But the hitherto-unrevealed fact is that fish can't tell the difference between an expensive fishing rod and a homemade fish pole! *And they couldn't care less.* So why not get a fish pole, and use all the money you save to buy lots of extra copies of this swell book to give to all your fishy friends?

"Yes, Twinky," exclaimed the enthusiastic young lad, "with a spot of luck, we'll fill our bag with perch from Poltroon Pond today! However, it will take a bit of doing; I'll hazard a guess that number eighteen sparsely hackled Bitch Creek Killers, tied onto 5X tippets and fished with a moderately slow retrieve may do the trick!"

"I just hope," replied Twinky, "that I get back in time to hide my nuts for the winter."

(CHAPTER CLXXVIII, p. 244, "The Liberated Squirrel.")

TRAGEDY AT ORVIS

Perils of piscatorial pursuits can oft extend to the maker, as well as the user, of fishing tackle. In 1822, giant nightcrawlers undermined the foundations of the Orvis Rod plant at Manchester, Vermont, causing the sickening collapse shown here. The company has since almost fully recovered from the setback.

WHAT

EVERY

YOUNG MAN

SHOULD

KNOW ☞

ABOUT FISHING RODS

If you insist on disregarding the wonderful advice proffered in the previous chapter, you ought to know a thing or two (2) about fishing rods before you go out and buy one (1). The following brief history of fishing rods tells all you need know:

Earliest Rods   Man's first fishing rods were made from wood. It soon became apparent that rods made from hickory, pine and oak were subject to dry rot and termite infestation. So no one caught any fish of any consequence.

Some companies tried building rods from bamboo, because termites could not stand its foul taste. However, Oriental gardeners soon seized the tip sections of bamboo rods for use as garden stakes. As a consequence, these rods never did catch on very well, and the people making bamboo rods decided to split.

The Cast-iron Rod   As available supplies of bamboo were diverted for use in breakfast cereal, metal rods came into being. However, a clever inventor named Gus Plumber put threads on the ends of the hollow rod sections and named them "pipe." This is how "plumbing" (named after the inventor) came into being. All metal rods were pre-empted for this use by the Army Engineers, and for several years fishermen had to stay home or be content with seining.

The Fibreglass Rod   Eight years later, Stanley Fibre and Livingstone Glass fortuitously met on the banks of the hippopotamus-infested Zambezi River, on the outskirts of Nairobi.

"Doctor Livingstone, I presume?" called out Stanley Fibre, in his now-famous words.

"Hell no!" cried Glass. "I'm not even the resident proctologist!" (Glass was known throughout East Africa for his merry wit.)

Glass and Fibre became fast friends and later pooled their knowledge to create the fibreglass rod. Parades and store-wide clearance sales were held to celebrate the historic event.

Space-age technologies have brought the fibreglass rod today to the point where it is impervious to mice, termites and fungi, and works every bit as good as the fishing pole.

"And if you listen intently," explained their fearless leader, drawing upon his inexhaustible knowledge of the wilderness and its curious ways, "you can hear the nightcrawlers breathing heavily as they relentlessly pursue their underground activities."
(CHAPTER LXXVII, p. 319, "Frankenstein
& the Wolf Man Meet Spiro Agnew.")

THE MIGHTY MISSISSIPPI

Few people are aware of the fact that the Mississippi River is man-made! Here Bob Cary ladles water which he has painstakingly carried in buckets from a lake near Ely, Minnesota, into the "source-slough." The water is then filtered through old beer cans, broken bottles, discarded foil and plastic wrap to make it fully compatible with "Old Man River's" other tributaries. Cary's lovely wife, Lil, chums the outflowing stream with lumps of chunk style peanut butter, which not only accounts for the characteristic discoloration of the Mississippi, but the effectiveness of bread as catfish bait, as well. The men in the background are professional worm diggers.

The Importance of Fish in One's Diet

Ear wax is not really wax at all, but one of the great many misnomers attributable to doctors. That stuff in your ears is really used-up brain cells, leaking out through your eustachian tubes. Unfortunately, it cannot be recycled. This is why fish in your diet are so important, since everyone knows fish are brain food. To replace your output of worn-out brain cells, you should eat at least 10 lbs. of codfish or mackerel every week. If you are not eating 10 lbs. of codfish or mackerel weekly, you are probably lots dumber than you even think.

HOW TO
IDENTIFY FISH GOOD

One of the first steps in learning how to fish good is that of recognizing different kinds of trout. The fact that not all trout are the same has led to the scientific conclusion that they are *different*. Learn these differences and you will be a better man for it. (Unless you are a woman.)

It is helpful to know that rainbow trout spawn in the spring, while brown trout spawn in the fall. Cutthroat trout, however, spawn whenever opportunity avails, so long as nobody is looking. This is all to the good; there is altogether too much immodesty in the world about us today.

Additionally, brown trout are fond of lying in shady spots. Rainbow trout, on the other hand, like to lie in bright sunshine. Trout fishermen are never fussy about where they lie. Listen for them in your neighborhood tackle shop.

Due to man's predations, many trout species have vanished forever. Gone are the precious jeweled fish from Oregon's Diamond Lake, as are the mildly laxative trout from Washington's Regulating Reservoir. And trout from Arizona's Virgin River, which never could be brought to reproduce, are today but a beautiful memory.

The famed feathered trout (below), found only in the West branch of the East Fork of the South Feather River in California, is today considered an endangered species. Fishermen must promptly put back any they catch. It is permissible, however, to remove one of the gaudy purple feathers from the caudal fin (which will soon grow back), as evidence of one's good fortune.

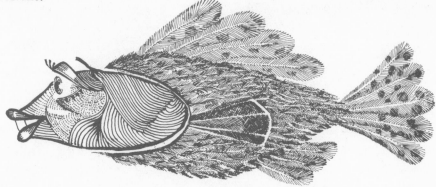

The year was 1812; the place, Rexburg, Idaho. Gifted young musical genius Wolfgang Green composed his celebrated "1812 Rexburg Overture" on his homemade fish flute. But orchestras everywhere refused to perform gifted young Wolfgang's opus, for fear that bones might become stuck in the flautists' throats. Downcast and discouraged, the gifted young genius said "Goodbye" to a musical career and became a worm breeder instead.

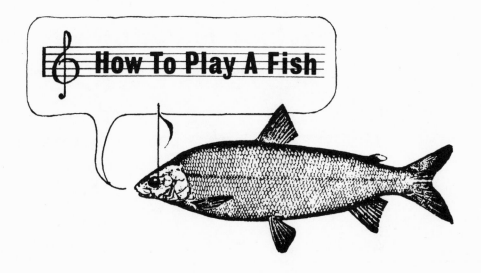

All shoddy books that attempt to deal with fishing fundamentals casually mention problems of (a) hooking the fish and (b) playing it. None until now have had the courage & candor to deal frankly with problems of "playing" the fish.

To play a fish, once you have it "on," requires skill & coordination, particularly where circumstances are involved. Begin by drilling holes in your mackerel approx. ½" apart. (If you have fat fingers, make this 1".) Finger it as you would a common piccolo. Begin with the scales, and take care not to get bones stuck in your throat.

An interesting combo can be put together with anglers performing on the guitar fish, drum fish and bass. One of the most-asked questions I receive is, "Should it be a string bass?" My answer is that I personally prefer 12 lb. test monofilament, but admittedly this is a subject not worth carping over.

*(No other book
on fishing has had either
the intelligence or the
courage, let alone both,
to tackle this
universal problem
up until now.)*

There are countless old wives' tales about how to release fishbones that get stuck in your throat. One can infer that old wives must be inordinately fond of eating fish. Why not ask if this is indeed so, when she comes home from work?

The best known folk remedy calls for simply swallowing a piece of bread. The idea is that the bread will act like a street sweeper, pushing everything in its path along with it. Just be careful not to use bread with a lot of holes in it. And avoid raisin bread. Raisins may get skewered on the fishbone, then you'll really be in trouble.

Once I was eating *mahi mahi* in a California cafe with Hilo Hattie. For the benefit of young whippersnappers who are ignorant of famous folk of yesteryear, Hilo Hattie was a reformed Hawaiian schoolteacher who sang with Harry Owens & His Royal Hawaiians. She was renowned for her original compositions ("When Hilo Hattie Does the Hilo Hop" made it up to #7 on the Hit Parade at one time).

But returning to our Golden State dining adventure, I managed to get a fishbone stuck in my throat, and began coughing loudly and banging things about.

"You are allergic to my grass skirt, no?" asked Hilo Hattie. "Or you have a fishbone stuck in your throat, yes?"

I nodded the appropriate choice.

"We native Hawaiians, of which regrettably few pure-blooded peoples, such as myself, still exist, are fortunately possessed of much ancient knowledge which is handed down from one generation to another, from mother to daughter, from father to son," Hilo thoughtfully explained as I clutched my throat and gasped for air. "Thus the wisdom of the ages flows down through the years. One such precious treasure of native lore deals with how to get fishbones unstuck from one's throat. It is very simple. It employs the timeless knowledge that bones have a magnetism, one for the other. Otherwise, how would our bodies hold together? It is because bones attract!"

She waggled a nicely tapered forefinger in my beet-red face to emphasize her point.

"All you need do," she explained, "is put another bone from the same fish atop your head! It will pull the bone in your throat loose!"

Having only seconds of life remaining, I was willing to try anything, however idiotic. I grabbed a handful of bones from my entree and whapped them atop my head.

Almost instantly my throat cleared.

"You see?" Hilo jubilated.

I have never satisfactorily solved the problem of how to get fishbones unstuck from one's hair.

The best solution of all to the stuck-fishbone problem is to order hamburger instead. This is also a wise conservation move. There is as yet no place where our native hamburger resource is threatened by the pollutions of industry, public utilities or the Army Corps of Engineers.

HOW TO
TELL LIES
GOOD

No one has figured out whether liars become fishermen, or fishermen turn into liars. There is a good deal of logic behind both theories, all of which are thoughtfully omitted from this good-taste book.

Everyone knows that only advertising copywriters lie as habitually as do fisherfolk. (The advertising copywriter who also fishes is indeed an awesome creature to behold.)

Since most fishermen use only standard, time-tested lies, we reveal some of the more prevalent prevarications, for the benefit of neophyte anglers:

1. "Me upset? Charlie, I'm *delighted* that you found this secret fishing hole, even though up until now I had it all to myself."
2. "I fish simply for relaxation. That's why I never feel the need to exaggerate."
3. "Charlie, I won't be the least bit upset if you catch a bigger fish today than I do."
4. "I'm strictly a fly fisherman. I've never stooped to worms and never will."
5. "Charlie, my heart is overflowing with joy because you caught this incredibly enormous fish here in my secret fishing hole. And on a worm, at that."
6. "I really don't care whether I catch any fish or not. The important thing is getting back to nature."
7. "No, I cannot understand why you got sick from those drinks I mixed, Charlie, and as a result are now critically ill with very low chances of survival."

OPENING DAY

George Washington was the only fisherman in all recorded
history who never told a lie, in order to preserve his public
image. He was notoriously unsuccessful as an angler, and

ON THE DELAWARE

it is believed that in the above classic picture depicting Washington opening the trout season on the Delaware, he instructed the artist to greatly exaggerate the size of the fish.

How To Learn About Fishing Conditions

In the photograph shown here, author Milford Poltroon is wearing his amazingly lifelike "Abe Lincoln" get-up. Poltroon has discovered that by wearing this original costume, while asking for advice in tackle shops, proprietors lie only ½ as often as otherwise, and even when they do, their lies are but ⅔ as untruthful as ordinarily.

It is proved fact, of course, that clerks in fishing tackle shops always direct people to the lousiest waters to be found within a 100-mile radius, so that on their day off they can enjoy the good streams and lakes without fear of dilution or contamination. But there are ways, known to experts, of breaking through this piscatorial pettifoggery. Kidnapping the shop-owner's youngest child, followed with a threatening ransom note, is no longer considered efficacious; most tackle shop proprietors are genuine conservationists, and believe that anything that will bring about a population cutback is all to the good. Simple, old-fashioned blackmail seldom works, either; storekeepers who openly sell Giant African Nightcrawlers and Rat-Faced MacDougals do not scare or embarrass easily.

If the already-described "Abe Lincoln" ploy fails to work, the author of this good-taste book recommends taking the tackle shop proprietor out and getting him drunk. When he is completely inebriated, get him out back of town and tie him securely to a stout tree. Next, give him a stiff shot of truth serum, and then take off his shoes and tickle the soles of his feet. Nine times out of ten, this methodology will make him talk. But watch out: he may lie.

ANNUAL MOTHER'S DAY SPAWNING RITES

Due to an unfortunate mixup, we are not sure whether this depicts the annual
Dolly Varden rites on the lower Madison, or Dolly Madison on the upper Varden.
(Despite the amazingly lifelike resemblance, the lady wearing the peace symbol
is not Jane Fonda.)

HOW TO
SPAWN

(The Fishfacts of Life)

Pacific salmon battle their way upstream for hundreds, sometimes thousands of miles, shunning food and drink en route, leaping high waterfalls, fighting perilous rapids, doing their damnedest to avoid all manner of obstacles and traps, ranging from nets and weirs to voracious grizzly bears and idiotic fishermen, and with the prospect of certain death awaiting at the end of their journey.

All this in order to spawn.

"Wow, man!" neophyte anglers are wont to exclaim, "Spawning must be a really cool scene, like WOW."

Is it?

The spawning act consists of the mama fish first knocking some rocks about with her tail, in order to make a nest. Then Pop and Mom lie alongside each other and wiggle. Then she lays her eggs. And Dad releases his milf (named after the author), which, as Ed Zern has pointed out, is inaccurately called *milt*.

That's all there is. There ain't no more.

Good grief, what a letdown! This is much worse than finding no prize in your Crackerjack box. Or finding no pot at the end of your rainbow.

It is thus evident that the "intelligence" of fish has not increased, over the millenniums of time, any more than that of fishermen.

Why

Fishermen Are Crazier Than Anybody

If you become a fisherman, you must resign yourself to the fact that neighbors, chance acquaintances and even "perfect" strangers will grin and snicker as you pass by, and ere long you will be known as a "character." Friends will make sport of you, jokes will be made at your expense; not very good ones, either. Worst of all, when you get sick, friends will send you dumb get-well cards with pictures of fish all over the outside. Some may even send you actual fish. Small wonder that most fishermen are an exceptionally healthy lot. The embarrassments accompanying illness are more than they can bear.

Eight years ago, the Eccentrics Evaluation League (EEL) did a depth study to determine whether fishermen or golfers were freakier. Everybody recognized that there was much to be said for both sides.

"Golfers," the research concluded, "spend hours knocking an inoffensive little ball over several miles of landscape, getting exhausted and often wet, dirty and numb in the process. Then they return home with nothing to show for their labors, other than a lot of alcohol on their breath.

"Fishermen, on the other hand, spend hours throwing an innocent, non-militant worm into Lake Fred, getting exhausted and often wet, dirty and numb in the process. Then they return home, usually with nothing to show for their labors and damaged equipment other than a lot of booze on their breath. *But sometimes (rarely) one will also bring back an uncleaned fish.*"

Why, then, are fishermen considered nuttier than golfers, particularly since amongst other lower animals, bringing back a "trophy of the chase" usually indicates a superior ability?

1. Because golf clubs don't smell up the house.
2. Because the golfer's wife never has to scale & clean a #4 iron.
3. Because the golfer doesn't sit around in non-golfing hours tying up sparsely hackled golf balls.
4. Because fishermen have been known willingly to pay up to $17,377.42 for travel expenses, lodging, gillies, pemmican, etc., in order to be able to stand in the middle of the famed Archnasty River in sub-zero temperatures, battling the strong current and with ice forming between the toes of the left foot due to leaky waders, with hideous gnawing pains in the stomach occasioned by the fact it was 8½ hours since breakfast and they forgot to bring a lunch, and with prospects of a 12-mile hike back to the lodge over a windswept high mountain pass frequented by grizzly bears and carnivorous meese . . . all for the privilege of heaving a $17 length of colored string into the numbing waters and then hauling it back in again, and repeating this idiotic process until something breaks or all their frozen fingers drop off into the river. And they call this "fun."

Those are 4 of the reasons why fishermen are crazier than anybody. We thoughtfully omit the other 96.

(We have just learned that the Montana State Golfing Commission is considering charging $15 for an annual golfing license. Proceeds will be used to stock the West Yellowstone course with fingerling golf balls.)

"Surprise!" cried brave 2nd Lieutenant Snav. "See what I caught on my sparsely hackled Unzippered Fly up on Maggie's Riffle!"

The girls could scarce contain their delight.

(CHAPTER Lxxviii, p. 342, "Orville K. Snav & His Giant Nightcrawler.")

Author Milford Poltroon fishes from a boat on a secluded mountain lake in the area of West Yellowstone, Montana. That this is indeed "Big Sky" country is attested to by the herds of geese, ducks, a box kite (serving as the transmitter for KOOK-TV in Billings), a 747 and an inspiring sunset, all simultaneously sharing the bustling atmosphere. Some potatoes from neighboring Idaho are to be seen in the foreground.

PAINTED BY FISHWORMS

This amazing work was done entirely by fishworms, who were taught to dip their tails in shoe polish and then crawl across a canvas in painstaking manner. This inspiring work teaches us that worms can be used for Good instead of Evil.

Why Fly Fishermen are big snobs

A single ounce of artificial flies can cost a fisherman as much as $617.45. Compare this with *real* flies, which presently go for a scant 35¢ per oz. at the West Yellowstone Memorial Garbage Dump. Or fishworms, which retail for 75¢ an ounce, in even the poshest nightcrawler boutiques.

This is proof aplenty that flyfishing offers enormous snob appeal. No honest angler can afford flyfishing, unless he steals his equipment. Your average fly man starts out, innocently enough, by purchasing one (1) dry fly for $3.75 plus tax. Little enough, you say. But then the unscrupulous bait shop proprietor informs him that he must also have a tapered leader to tie the fly to ($37.20), a creel ($95), a guide dog ($2.98), a wading staff ($77.25), plus a rod, line, whisky glasses, ice cubes, waders, hat, vest, poker chips, score pads, pencil sharpener, together perhaps with some optional equipment, and he has spent a minimum of $17,893.14 before he knows it! And that's just the beginning.

The fantastic expense of flyfishing is but one of its snob appeals. Another is the invitation it offers to become absorbed in semi-related trivia.

Some years ago, while working up a pool on the Brodheads in Pennsylvania, I chanced across another angler, who, rather than sensibly fishing, had his rod leaned up against a tree and was kneeling alongside the streambank, staring at some microscopic flotsam through a magnifying glass. When I asked, *he confessed to be studying the lower abdomen of the female caddis fly!* You can be sure I got out of there fast, having had brushes with sex perverts before. Only a male caddis fly would have a normal, wholesome interest in the lower abdomen of a female caddis fly. And he was not.

Abnormal, unwholesome interests in peripheral issues, like the sex life of bugs, are common amongst flyfisherfolk, however. You'll never find a good hardware fisherman wasting valuable hours studying metal alloys. And no good worm dunker has ever authored a treatise on the sex life of the Arizona wiggler. Only flyfishermen are devotees of non-fishing.

On the plus side, however, is the undisputed fact that flycasting is ridiculously easy, as the accompanying illustration makes abundantly evident. Fly men are also more liberal when mixing drinks for their friends and, in keeping with their snob image, more prone to serve higher-priced, higher proof booze. And a bucketful of artificial flies, when inadvertently left in the car trunk for a week, will not smell objectionable in the least.

Being able to flycast good doesn't constitute the whole of fly fishing, by a long shot. Even though Bing McClellan of Traverse City, Michigan, can line out a 1,487-foot cast effortlessly, as he is shown doing here, strangely enough he has yet to catch his first fish.

LEXICON OF FLY FISHING

The use of improper language on a trout stream is as rasping to the sensitive, well-shaped ears of the experienced fly fisherman as is the sour note to the professional musician, or the engine knock to the race driver. So that the fly fishing novice need not suffer embarrassment, we present the following lexicon of fly fishing terminology and urge that you commit it to memory:

WE DON'T SAY:	WE DO SAY:
FISH POLE	FLY ROD
STRING	LINE
SPOOL	REEL
HOOK	FLY
BITE	STRIKE
SPIKKLED TROUT	BROOK TROUT
THEM PURTY FISH	RAINBOW TROUT
THEM MEAN-LOOKIN BASTIDS	BROWN TROUT
RUBBER PANTS	WADERS
SACK	CREEL
SIEVE	NET
SHUCKS	GODDAM
GOSHDARN	GODDAM
O PSHAW	O PSHIT

Famous Insects After Which Fishing Flies Are Named

(1) BAR FLY or Olive Spinner
(2) WOOLLY WORM or Harry Thing
(3) BLUE UPRIGHT or Fuzz
(4) HOUSE FLY (with house)
(5) DAMSEL or Mayfly Nymph
(6) CADDIS (male caddie)
(7) HOPPER (just hopped)

WORLD'S FIRST

The world's first slot machine was invented in West Yellowstone, Montana, in 1812 by the famous Harold Slot, insurance man & gambling hall proprietor. In the above photo the historic first model is being operated by the notorious Madame Discount, colorful W. Yellowstone society figure who later fell into disrepute when

milford poltroon

FISHSLOT MACHINE

she overtly attempted to start a local branch of the PTA. (Even
unto this day, left-wing organizations are frowned upon in &
around West Yellowstone.) Slot's first machine was later outmoded
by improved models that dispensed coins rather than hatchery
trout, and that did not require a horse to pull the handle.

RIDING THE BAIT BUCKET

Bringing up giant worms from the historic West Yellowstone Nightcrawler Mines was indeed a hazardous task, and brave were the men who rode the bait bucket down the 600-foot shaft. Today the abandoned mine serves as a storage well for the brown gravy served in West Yellowstone cafes.

HOW TO

INVENT FIRE

Experienced fishermen have learned that when one falls in a river or lake, one gets "wet." All too frequently, this is considered an unpleasant sensation, particularly if the thermometer hovers around the freezy point. Thus fishermen have learned, over the centuries, that it is desirable to rid themselves of this shivery-damp sensation by means of "heat."

In urban areas, "heat" may be produced by a variety of sophisticated goods, i.e., electric blankets, freshly cooked oatmeal, gas furnaces and diggety dogs. (It was from the latter that today's popular phrase, "Hot Diggety Dog!" sprung.) But in wild areas where fish lurk, such modern conveniences seldom abound. So it is good to know some backwoods ways of creating "heat."

Matches are swell, having been invented by Closecover Beforestriking in 1802, for the express purpose of fire starting. However, fishermen have found that when matches get "wet," they will not ignite (light). And waterproof containers for matches always leak.

So if caught in a situation outdoors where you hunger for heat, look first to see if sun (big glarey thing up in sky) is out. If yes, this connotes it is "daytime," but do not look for help to the television networks, whose programs are notoriously hideous during daylight hours. Instead, look for something that can magnify and concentrate the sun's rays on navel lint or other tender tinder. The lens from your watch (assuming you know how to tell time), your camera, flashlight, or even your eyeglasses will work. Even hunks of ice from frozen ponds have been used to start fires this way.

Another good way to start fires it to wait for a thunderstorm and then run about wrapped in galvanized chicken wire. And some fishermen, with diligent practice, learn how to combust spontaneously. If all else fails, try leaving the iron plugged in.

In early Roman times, anglers always baited their fly with a bit of anchovy pizza, such as we see Tricia Caesar holding in her left hand. (The design of chest waders has been remarkably improved since then.)

TRAGIC CONSEQUENCES
OF
FISHING IGNORANCE

When Caesar crossed the Rubicon in 49 B.C., he paused and said, "Yonder pools may harbor trout-fish. Let us try a few casts!"

"Wet fly or dry?" asked Cassius.

"Dry," advised Caesar, and *the dry was cast*. An over-eager reporter wrote it down as *the die is cast*, thus confusing countless generations of Latin students.

Fish drink water only when they have no choice

A distillery accidentally leaked some whiskey into the River Endrick in Scotland and astonished anglers saw salmon and trout weaving drunkenly through the stream, snapping carelessly at hooks.

This item appeared as a United Press International release in newspapers throughout the U.S. not too long ago.

I have long been aware of the fact that fish share the fisherman's love of the Cup That Cheers. I have used this knowledge to great advantage. I have observed, however, that most fishermen are unwilling to SHARE. And they come staggering home with empty creels. This serves them right.

Many years ago, while fishing the Madison River, I slipped on a submerged banana peel. The flask of snake repellent I providently carried in my hip pocket burst asunder; the entire contents leached through my red flannel underwear into the river. I managed to escape from the enormous cutthroat trout, or "Montana piranha" as they are better known, in the nick of time.

This was the beginning of my high-proof research into behavior patterns of fish, when they are allowed to drink something other than plain branch water.

One highly effective angling methodology is to empty a fifth of booze directly into the water. Fish downstream from the emptying point. Highly educated browns appear to favor Jack Daniel's Old No. 7 Black Label, while more naive rainbows and cutthroats exhibit a marked preference for martinis. To properly chill the martinis, introduce a truckload of ice cubes into the laughing waters. If waters are not laughing at the outset, wait 5 minutes and listen for snickers. Fish with an upright Olive Fly, heavily hackled with a twist of lemon.

A by-product of this research has been the discovery of the way to make the world's driest martini:

Empty a full bottle of vermouth into the river. Save the bottle. At a point 5 miles or more downstream from the emptying point, refill the bottle with the same vermouth, which by now has been properly thinned. Freeze the contents in refrigerator trays, and use these cubes to chill your martini glasses. Discard the vermouth cubes just before filling the glasses with unadulterated gin.

MESSINA, GODDESS OF WRETCHEDNESS

According to the lovely legend in ancient Pocatello mythology, Messina fell in love with Klein, god of cut-rate chest waders. Together they spent six years fishing the Styx during the Mayfly hatch, but with poor results, due to sloppy casting, leaky waders, etc. Domestic difficulties thus ensued.

It is believed the fish held by Messina in the classic picture shown here is a fake, cleverly dubbed in by Instamatic, god of photography, who was her secret lover.

DEBBIE MEDUSA

For many years Debbie Medusa was one of West Yellowstone, Montana's, most popular Society figures. Yet Debbie had nightcrawlers for hair. Dermatologists diagnosed this strange condition as arising from acute dandruff conditions, coupled with the fact that Debbie's mother had been frightened by a worm fisherman during pregnancy. Local hairdressers were baffled by Debbie's tresses, and she came to rely almost entirely on home permanents. Even these left much to be desired, and she thus yearned for the day when the Toni Company might merge with Carter's Worm Farm, combining their knowledge for a better worm world.

In 1947 Debbie eloped with a Pocatello bait dealer and has not been heard from since.

"Yes, Twinky," exclaimed bright-eyed little Jack, "we'll catch a falling star! And from it we'll fashion a gossamer thing of such magic, that the sparkling trout in yon crystal stream cannot resist its mystic enchantment!"

"It embarrasses me," replied Twinky, "when people mistake me for Spiro Agnew."

(Vol. III, Chapter CCLXVI, p. 198, "Fishing the Gossamer Nymph.")

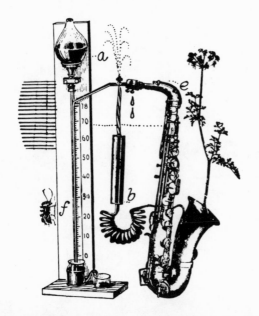

BUSH COMBING

Years ago, when I first started fly fishing, I snagged and lost many artificial flies on streamside bushes, because of my sloppy backcast. I reasoned that scores . . . nay, hundreds! . . . of other fisherfolk must, on occasion, do the same thing. If my reasoning was correct, this would mean that every streamside willow and alder must be festooned with countless trout flies. But since their color camouflage and tiny size makes them well-nigh invisible, how could they be retrieved?

This line of forceful, constructive thinking led to the invention of my unique bush comb, a clever instrument designed for gently combing foliage of all sorts, leaving leaves and blossoms intact, but gingerly removing all artificial flies.

My first use of this handsomely crafted tool proved the soundness of my theory. From a single bush I retrieved 3 Royal Coachman bucktails, 5 Rat-faced MacDougals, 3 Cowdungs, 10 Colorado Spinners, 2 striped bass jigs and 7 quarts of delicious wild choke cherries.

While my bush comb is as yet the only one of its kind, you may easily fashion one for yourself by merely duplicating the simple model illustrated above. The only materials needed are a few harp strings, an empty bed pan and any good used automatic wart remover (not the Butane model).

FRIGHTFUL FISHPUZZLE

Boy, what a bunch of dumb-looking fish, eh? With a well-sharpened pencil, try to connect all the fish with four straight lines, without lifting your writing instrument from the paper, crossing any lines or going out for a beer. Answer on page 128.

HOW TO AVOID

FISH-FRIGHT

Have you never heard of "fish-fright?" You are not alone. Neither had your fish-minded author until this news story appeared in the daily papers a while back:

HONOLULU (AP)—A Los Angeles man and woman who went to the South Pacific seeking an island paradise returned to Honolulu Saturday after a "frightening" 40 days on a small Fijian Island.

Bruce Johnson, a 42-year-old health enthusiast, said the paradise turned out "much more rugged than we anticipated."

He and Shari Quam, 22, originally had planned to spend several months on an uninhabited island near Samoa. The couple said their Robinson Crusoe adventure turned out to be a "horrible" experience.

Johnson said, "There was nothing there—nothing. Just coconuts and crabs. That is what we lived on."

The two declined to discuss their more frightening moments on the island. Johnson said only that they experienced an instance of "fish-fright." They took with them only fishing gear and swimming suits, hoping to live off the land and seas.

Deeply moved by this accounting, I promptly wrote to a number of fish authorities of one sort or another. What, I asked, was this unexplained "fish-fright?" Did a shark bark? A tigerfish snarl? Did they inhale deadly bass gas?

The eminent Dr. Meyer Friedman, director of the Harold Brunn Institute at Mt. Zion Hospital in San Francisco and a man who favors dry flies, answered:

Dear Milford:
There are no medical articles concerning "fish-fright" as such. How about having lunch next week?

Dr. George Martin of Redding, California, replied as follows:

Dear Milf:
I don't know anything about fish fright and I don't want to know anything about it. What do you expect out of a health enthusiast? Yours for more less fatal diseases.

John Zervas, Director of the American Fishing Tackle Manufacturers Association in Chicago, was most constructive:

Dear Milf:
Unrequited love on South Sea islands can lead to what natives refer to as the "Fiji Fidgets," or "Fijits," as it is transliterated in the islands. When the sweating swain is repulsed by a maiden who menaces him with a malodorous mackerel, he may be impelled to climb a coconut tree out of "piscaphobia," which the old (and young) Romans recognized as "fish-fright."

And R. W. Prichard in the North Carolina *Medical Journal* apparently solved the problem when he wrote:

Dear Assorted Poltroons:
"Fish-Fright," has been a recognized disease here since Pocahontas told her boyfriend about it. Simply put, it is an annual disorder of the earthworm (*L. terrestrus*) occurring about April 1, and lasting until Labor Day, consisting of fear, trembling, morbid thoughts of drowning, etc.
Call me anytime.

Henry Wadsworth ("Lefty") Poltroon, famed poet and angler of Two Dot, Montana, with his loyal, inseparable companion, "Lassie."

Botticelli Poltroon

OPENING DAY

Paula Revere, popular waitress at West Yellowstone's A & W Drive-in, helps inaugurate the opening of trout season on famed Henry's Lake, in neighboring Idaho. On the right, Mrs. Pat Barnes demonstrates a new brand of

ON HENRY'S LAKE

water-resistant tarpaulins now stocked at Barnes' Tackle Shop in West Yellowstone. The couple on the left are believed to be conducting market research for a new breath sweetener.

While President Andrew Jackson (shown here with an average day's catch) was a devoted fisherman, he did not believe in "catch and release." Known to the public as "Old Hickory," his angling cronies knew him better as "Old Split Bamboo" (but never, contrary to rumor, as "Old Fibreglass").

Our Piscatorial Presidents

There are more fishermen in the U.S.A. than anything, including baseball buffs, television repair men, used car dealers and even fish. Small wonder that smart-brained Presidents and candidates for this well-paying office have long realized the publicity value of being shown fondling fishing rods. This can reel in a lot of votes.

The first President to take advantage of this fishfact was none other than G. Washington himself, today revered as the Fishfather of our Country. In the rare engraving back there on page 32, George is seen hooked into a 5 lb. 6 oz. cutthroat trout in the Delaware River. (The gunk cluttering the water is not floating globs of detergent foam, as would be the case today, but nice old-fashioned ice.)

Many subsequent Presidents and Vices have been sporty-type anglers of one sort or another. Both Theodore and Franklin D. Roosevelt enjoyed frothing up waters, Teddy preferring wilderness streams while F.D.R. was an Atlantic boat troller, in the main. Herbert Hoover was a flyfishing nut, and particularly fond of the McKenzie River, out Oregon way. He even found time to write a little book titled, "Fishing for Fun and to Wash Your Soul." Eisenhower, too, liked high mountain trout streams, while John F. Kennedy was mostly a salt-water fisherman.

It is significant that neither Nixon nor Agnew has been photographed holding fish poles. Small wonder that our country is going to Hell in a handbasket.

HOW TO

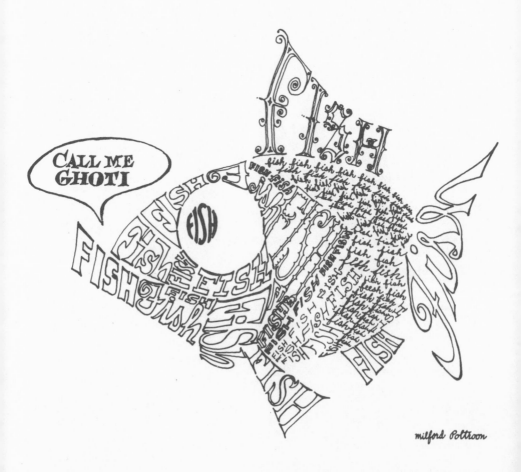

SPELL A FISH

Every so often, some smartass newspaper columnist points out that *ghoti* spells fish, and makes it abundantly clear that he thinks he is clever as all billy damn in so doing.

Bah.

Forty-seven years back, George Bernard Shaw figured out that ghoti spells fish. Pronounce the GH as in LAUGH, the O as in WOMEN, the TI as in NATION. It all adds up to FISH.

Mr. Shaw used this as an example of the absurdities of the English language.

There are, of course, lots of other swell ways to spell fish.

For example:

PHUSI: pronounce the PH as in PHYSIC, the U as in BUSY, and the concluding SI as in PENSION.

FFESS: pronounce the FF as in OFF, the E as in PRETTY, and the double S as in PASSION, which you are doubtlessly filled with by now.

UGHYCE: pronounce the UGH as in ENOUGH, the Y as in HYMN, and the CE as in OCEAN. The ocean is full of ughyces.

So next time you see some lard-brained newspaper columnist taking credit for discovering that *ghoti* spells fish, you may want to write a letter and remind him of the homey backwoods wisdom my grandmother taught me many years ago when she dandled me on her knee:

Nobody likes a smartass.

HOW TO TELL

FISH JOKES
GOOD

The world's worst jokes, countless in number, invariably deal with the timeless problem of finding a fly in one's soup in a public dining place. Samples of the best (or worst) known:

Waiter! There's a fly in my soup.
Don't worry, sir. It won't eat much.

Waiter! What's this fly doing in my soup?
I believe he's skinnydipping, sir.

Waiter! There's a fly in my soup!
You're mistaken, sir. That's a cockroach.

With a modicum of thought, fly-in-the-soup jokes can be easily fisherman-oriented. Revolting examples:

Waiter! What's this fly in my soup?
It looks like a #16 Wulff-tied Royal Coachman to me, sir.

Waiter! There's a fly in my soup.
Yes, sir. The Washington Fly Fishing Club is here tonight.

Waiter! How did this fly get in my soup?
Sir, to properly understand, you must have at least a rudimentary knowledge of the entomological process involved. The eggs, which the adult female deposits on the soup's surface, sink to the bottom and there, amongst the noodles, hatch into nymphs. These spend the fall and winter months feeding on such organic detritus as the soup may contain, along with the noodles. Then, in the springtime, the nymphal skin splits, and the first winged stage emerges amongst the rich chunks of hearty beef. Twenty-four hours later the skin is shed again—some of our patrons, in fact, are fond of calling this "skin soup"—and the fully mature insect appears amongst the croutons. That is what you are observing now. Did you have any other questions, sir?

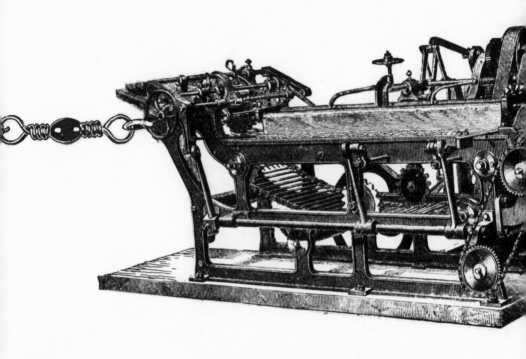

MURCHISON'S

Seven-tenths of the earth's surface is covered with water.

If there were as many different kinds of fish as there are fishing lures, this would have to be enlarged to ten or eleven-tenths, in order to hold just one pair of each.

The limitless variety of colors, shapes, sizes, textures and gonkyness of fishing lures obtainable in a well-stocked tackle shop, is enough to boggle the mind of the most boggle-proof angler today. Some of the larger trolling lures use considerably more metal, glass and upholstering than today's more popular imported sport cars, and are comparably priced.

The reason, of course, for this ever-continuing proliferation of hardware is the fisherman's eternal hope that some new combination of beads, bangles and metal alloys will prove to be the magic Infallible Fish Eradicator. So far as the fish themselves are concerned, they'd be happy and content

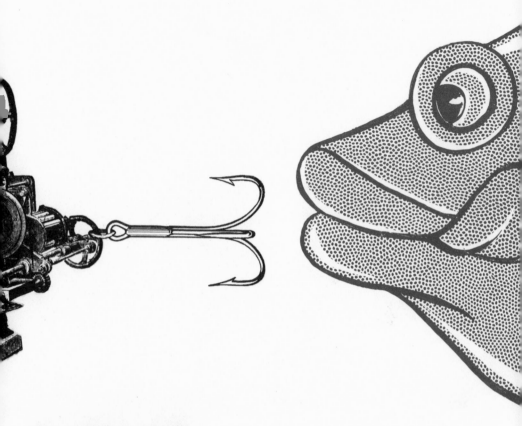

KILLER

if lures were cut back to not more than 2 or 3 varieties, available only in standard colors and flavors.

The earliest known trout lure, "Murchison's Killer," was created in 1776 for trolling in Yellowstone Lake. Highly favored by local meat fishermen, it gradually lost popularity as larger and more sophisticated lures came into being. When Claude Duncan first opened his West Yellowstone hardware store in 1832, his entire inventory consisted of hardware dredged from the bottoms of nearby lakes and streams.

Even today, when storm winds blow and the waves churn high, the clanking and banging together of large lumpy lures that line bottoms of all local waters can be heard for miles around. Easily mistaken for church bells, this tintinnabulation often engenders temporary pious feelings in local fisherfolk. Recovery from such is usually quite rapid, however.

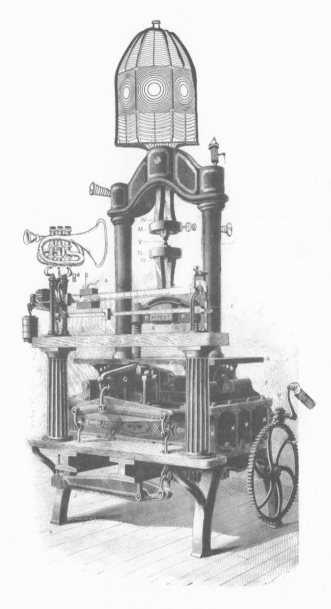

FIG. I

HOW THE
SPINNING REEL
EVOLVED

To completely understand how anything works, you must know the history of it. Like your wife. (Assuming she works.) The same basic scientific principle applies to fishing gear. But how much do you *really* know about your rod, reel, line and lures?

The answer, of course, is nothing.

To overcome your handicap, let's begin with the spinning reel.

The first spinning reel (FIG. I) was invented by Ely Smut, a pioneer worm fisherman, in 1829. Operated by steam, the reel, while revolutionary in theory, proved unsatisfactory in actual use, due to a tendency of the steam combustion boilers to explode as fish were being reeled in. A lesser drawback was the fact that the reel weighed 947 lbs., making it unsuitable for most light tackle fishing.

Today's spinning reel has overcome over 87% of the problems described. Shown (FIG. II) is Garcia's Model #3347-2J04A-0013S52-882M01-4P8205.

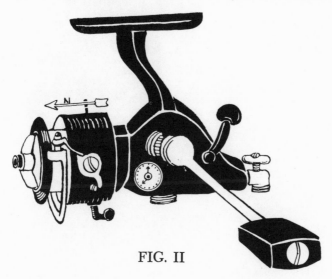

FIG. II

PEACHES
PFLUEGER

Billed as the "Revolving
Wench," Peaches Pflueger
was the top attraction of
nightclubs in Montana's
panhandle, in the late
1800's. The ravishing Miss
Pflueger originated a
dance wherein, as she
twirled with dervish-like
speed, she wound an
HDH double-tapered fly-
line around her mid-
section. Inspired by her
terpsichorean talents,
makers of the first fishing
reels called their products
"revolving wenches."
Newspaper typesetters,
however, corrupted this to
"winches" and later to
"reels" (the latter was not
easy).

Why Trout Meat from some Trout has a Different Color than Meat from some other Trout

People often ask, "Why is it that some trout have white meat and others have meat that is pink?"

The answer is that trout meat color, which can range from snow white to rose red, is determined by these factors:

1. Political affiliations.
2. What they've been feeding on.
3. Emotional instability. Some blush more easily than others.
4. What they've been feeding on.
5. Environmental factors.
6. What they've been feeding on.

Thus trout feeding on pistachio ice cream and cucumber rinds invariably have green meat. And hatchery trout, which everywhere are fed a diet of polished rice and uncolored marshmallows, have ghastly white flesh.

Hatchery trout also have rounded tails, which come from batting them against the sides of the cement troughs where they hang out, and are thus easy to tell from the sharp-tailed and -witted native trout.

Take
a Fish
Fishing

Every year more than 37,378,151 Americans go a-fishing in our rivers, swamps, lakes and other moist places where finny creatures may lurk. Why?

Meat is one answer. Success for such folk is measured solely by quantities of dead fish fetched home in the gunny sack or creel.

Exercise is another.

"A man your age, Roy, needs plenty of exercise," your doctor finger-waggles. "Fishing is fine exercise. Brings all the muscles into play. Gets you out where you breathe air, not this muck here in the city. Go fishing, Roy."

For this advice your doctor bills $37.50. Thus by the time you buy a cheap rod, reel, line and other needfuls ($375.98 additional), you are in too deep to back out.

You go fishing.

A third motivation for fishing is the excitement of simply catching

fish, whether or not any energies are expended. By using marvelous new boons to mankind, such as transistorized fish finders, electric reels, unbreakable hawsers and such, virtually all physical effort may be successfully avoided.

But the strongest reason of all for fishing is the hope of catching a fish while another fisherman is watching. This is sound scientific fact. Whenever an experienced angler is fast to a fighting fish, his first move is to look about to see if anybody is watching.

If the fisherman discovers he has an audience, joy reigns unconfined. He heaves, sweats, struggles, groans, curses and otherwise makes it evident that this is a Fish Battle of the Century, to be won only through enormous skill. But if no one else is nigh, the fish is landed in a tenth of the time it otherwise takes, with little if any joy for either fisherman or fish.

As further proof, here's what several world-renowned fishermen report on this matter:

"Once on the Overkill, I hooked into a 4½-inch plant trout just as some dumb kid came around the bend upstream. Through deft footwork, running rapidly downstream and screaming at the top of my voice, I made that dumb kid think I was into a 10-pounder. What a thrill!"

E. Z., Theodore Gordon Flyfishers

"If I get a good fish on and no one is around to watch, I break down and cry like a goddam baby."

B. M., Traverse City, Michigan

"Years back, fishing the Kispiox for lunker steelhead, I had no success for 6 days handrunning. Then just as another fisherman broke through the brush, I managed to hook into a small sculpin. I immediately dashed into the stream to the point where the waters began flooding into my chest waders. "GO GET HELP!" I screamed to the wide-eyed onlooker. When he ran to do so, I recovered myself. I later used the sculpin for bait, albeit unsuccessfully. What a wonderful day!"

S. R., Washington Fly Fishing Club

" Once on the Trinity in California, I was into a steelhead that later weighed in at 22 lbs., 14 oz. Even though I prolonged the fight for a good two hours and a half, not a soul showed up to watch. I was so downcast I went home and beat hell out of my wife and dog."

F. G., Long Beach Flycasters

Having thus learned that the supreme moment in angling is the time of being observed in mid-fight, I have learned the sure-fire secret of angling success:

Take a fish fishing!

I have arrangements with a leading fish market on San Francisco's Fisherman's Wharf to ship me a frozen starry-eyed flounder every day of the fishing season. (Sally Riley, West Yellowstone's beloved postmaster, can vouch for the truth of this statement.) And every day, as I sally 4th * on the Yellowstone, Madison or other favored local water, I carefully tuck my daily flounder into a pocket in my fishing vest.

I never fish a stretch of river without first making sure another fisherman is close at hand. Then I carefully affix my flounder to favored fly, toss it into the waters and let the current take it downstream. Then WHANGO, GOOMBAH, ZAP, HOOHA! The fight is on! It is truly amazing how a dead flounder can, when properly drifted in a strong current, give a lifelike illusion of battling to the utmost!

When, at long last, the spent fish is finally brought to net, some smart-assed onlooker will occasionally say, "I didn't know there were any starry-eyed flounders in the Yellowstone River."

I look such people piercingly in the eye and say, "You got a lot to learn about fishing, buddy boy."

The true secret of angling success is to take a fish fishing.

---

* Sally often follows with a 5th.

Lots of books on fishing tell you how important it is to

LEARN HOW TO BACKCAST

but not one in a hundred tells you how to do it. So here expert flycaster Frank Gray takes time off from instructing at the Fenwick School of Fly Fishing in West Yellowstone to demonstrate the right way to handle your backcast. First, lie on your back. Second, cast in normal, ordinary fashion. Third, as the line goes zinging out, arch your back (SEE PHOTO) and deliver the full power thrust through your elbows.

81

"ALMOST HAD HIM!"

Those were the words of Billy Graham-cracker, Religion & Bingo Editor of the Wretched Mess News. "It was on the South Fork last Tuesday just below Maggie's Riffle, when he hit. He'd of gone this long easy, but a vicious woodpecker bit the line in two, just as I was about to land him. I was downcast but my faith sustained me."

FISHING FOR AVIDS

If you read *Outdoor Sports Afield & Stream* and other fish-oriented magazines, you know that anglers are invariably referred to as "avid fishermen." The term is a corruption of "Avis fishermen," which originated as follows:

Back in 1897, a brilliant investment counselor and blackjack dealer by the name of Fred Avis settled in the little community that was laughingly known as "West Yellowstone," Montana. Observing the steady flow of frustrated fishermen who passed through the village, Fred Avis opened the first Rent-a-Fish agency. Anglers who got skunked after a day of frothing up the Madison River could discreetly rent a limit of lunker trout from Avis, and thus have a creelful of conversation pieces to exhibit while making the the late-afternoon tour of the local saloons.

The business folded some years later when Avis made the mistake of renting a fish that had over 1,000 miles on its odorometer.

BRINGING HOME

THE DAY'S CATCH

In the early days of fishing in the vicinity of West Yellowstone, no good sport ever kept a fish that weighed less than 400 lbs. The only practical way to fetch home fish of this size, and upward, was to fit it with wheels and hitch it to a team of horses.

These rigs, manufactured by Irving Chrysler of Rigby, Idaho, soon became known as "Chrysler's imperial way of bringing home fish."

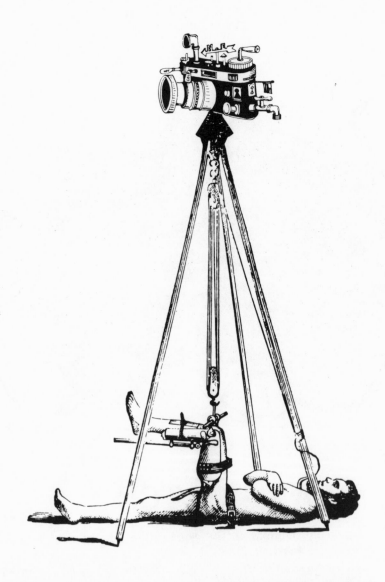

Just because a camera has a lot of fancy gizmos and extras and maybe even a remote-control mechanism is no guarantee it will take better pictures, so watch out.

HOW TO COPE WITH EVIL SPIRITS THAT LURK IN CAMERAS

Back in 1963, an enlightening article that appeared in the *Wretched Mess News* contained this paragraph:

> *DO NOT photograph fishermen and other natives of West Yellowstone, Montana, without first obtaining their permission. Many are superstitious about "evil spirits" lurking in cameras.*

Readers wrote into inform us that this belief is not confined to tribes in West Yellowstone, but is shared by aborigines in the Australian outback, jungle folk of Tasmania and an estimated 37.2% of people living in the suburbs of St. Louis, Missouri.

Accordingly, the *Wretched Mess News*, always anxious to seek out the truth, conducted exhaustive research into the matter.

Our conclusions:

> *Only the earliest Instamatics, all Leicas made prior to 1922 and the Farkel with the f1.9 wide-angle lens have evil spirits.*

All other makes are 100% safe, and may be used for photographing any fish you may catch, with impunity.

A WORD IN DEFENSE OF THE
ARMY
CORPS OF
ENGINEERS

Fishermen and conservationists are all too prone to criticize the Army Corps of Engineers, simply because this hard-working group is constantly striving to dam all the rivers and streams in this country.

In a recent lecture given to the West Yellowstone Garbage Improvement League, Col. Elmo Crossrib, who holds a high post (not shown) with the Engineers, defended Corps policy:

"We have proved irrefutably that running water carries germs and bacteria. In addition, immoral acts have been known to take place on streams and rivers, in rowboats, canoes and even on barges. Therefore, we make every effort to hastily dam it up, in our unceasing efforts to stamp out germs, bacteria and immorality."

THE
BLACK
HOLE
OF
WEST YELLOWSTONE

Apart from the interior and exterior, little remains of the infamous prison that once shamefully blotted the escutcheon of West Yellowstone, Montana, and which drew censure from humanitarians, conservationists and phrenologists the world over. The mainstream of criticism was not directed at the feeding of the prisoners, which admittedly was not too bad, embracing, as it did, a 7-course dinner with champagne, served by ravishing waitresses, plus a Saturday-night barbecue and dance. Similarly, the housing facilities—room service, valet, barber, etc.—were generally conceded to be only slightly below U.S. standards. The critics, however, full of righteous anger, pointed out that while inmates could easily observe fish leaping in the nearby Madison River, the prison grounds were completely lacking in trout fishing ponds, streams or fishing facilities of any kind! Giving in, finally, to pressures from the Civil Fish Liberties Union, the prison was abandoned and later converted into the Sleepy Hollow Motel.

Undersized tangerines, as shown by the waitress in this photo, were yet another reason why the early West Yellowstone prison drew censure.

"Yes sir, Fletcher," cried the rising young advertising agency's President, "I'll kiss your bass if that isn't the biggest fish I ever saw come out of Gumfudgin Creek!" "I'll drink to that!" exclaimed the friendly visiting lady evangelist.

(Vol. III, Part 2, Chap. Clxxviii, "Secrets of Nymph Fishing")

HOW TO
SURVIVE
GOOD
IN THE
WILDERNESS

Could you survive on the fish you catch the next time you get hopelessly lost in the wilds? Your problem stems from the fact that you'd need a minimum of 4,500 calories a day, yet your average 1-pound rainbow trout has only about 200 calories. So you'd have to catch and eat 22½ one-pound trout every day. Not only would you be exceeding legal creel limits and thus subjecting yourself to fine and possible imprisonment if a game warden catches you, but it is highly unlikely that a person such as yourself could catch anywhere near this amount, even if you lie.

One solution is to go after fat fish, which are much higher in calories. Trout that live principally on marshmallows, jelly beans and Velveeta cheese, as do all those within 23 miles of West Yellowstone, often go as high as 1977½ calories per pound.

But an even better solution is one I figured out all by myself. Calorie tables show that while an outdoorsman may burn up 600 calories per hour, your average incompetent office worker can get by on fewer than 50 c.p.h.! The answer is obvious: always take along plenty of office work when the slightest danger of getting lost exists. But don't make the mistake, as I did at first, of taking an electric typewriter unless you also have an extremely long extension cord.

DO THEY CALL YOU "OLD DUMBNUTS?"

One way you can avoid being called embarrassing, distasteful names is to always remember to take along the right gear. The angler shown here, who shall mercifully remain nameless, has made the dumb mistake of bringing a net several sizes too small for a stream like the upper North Fork, where large trout are not uncommon.

ARE
TROUT
AS
SMART

AS

YOU

ARE

?

While a trout's brain is smaller than that of the average trout fisherman's, it is of much higher quality and capable of higher performance at faster speeds. In one of the most innovative of transplant operations, a group of surgeons at West Yellowstone's Veterans and Veterinary Hospital last year succeeded in exchanging the brains of a 16-pound cutthroat trout and a 160-pound trout fisherman. In studying the habits of both following the operation, it was noted that the trout took to muddying up the water, left cans and bottles lying about, made loud unpleasant guttural noises and was given to lecherous spawning at odd hours. On the other hand, the trout fisherman who was given the cutthroat's brain became very shy, and took to hiding behind large rocks for most of the daylight hours. In the evening, however, he was fond of coming out and leaping from time to time.

PRATT'S CENTRIFUGAL RADIATING FISH KILLER

Invented in 1911 by Albert Pratt of Woodinville, Washington, the Centrifugal Radiating Fish Killer utilized, for the first time in history, the tremendous latent energy in canned meat balls. By simply turning a hand crank to release the radiating dynamic power rays, the operator could infallibly kill fish as he merely walked across the surface of the lake or stream. Because of certain problems overlooked by the inventor, however, Pratt's Centrifugal Radiating Fish Killer never wholly succeeded.

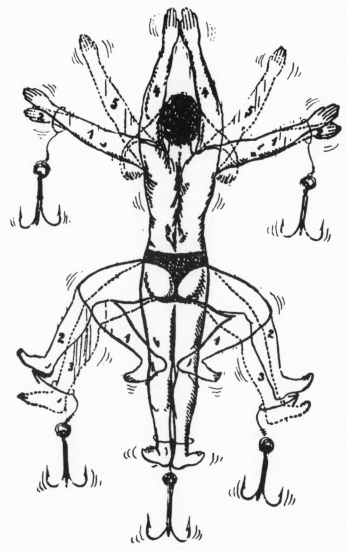

POLTROON'S MAGIC INFALLIBLE FISH LURE

The lure shown here is one I invented all by myself and which I offer to any opportunity-minded manufacturer of fishing lures. Naturally, I expect a pile of money for it.

The incredible flexo-action 5-position slithering undulating lure imitates the *exact* movements of a WORM FISHERMAN! It is thus guaranteed to arouse the anger,. deep-seated hatred and fighting instincts of game fish throughout! Available with double, quadruple or 149 treble hooks (weedless) in authentic worm fisherman colors: puce, brindle and bile green.

Great Fishthoughts of Western MAN

"Though a man eat fish till his guts crack, yet if he eat no flesh he fasts."
JOHN TAYLOR, 1630

"What an idiot is man to believe that abstaining from flesh, and eating fish, which is so much more delicate & delicious, constitutes fasting."
NAPOLEON I, 1817

"Fish must swim thrice — once in the water, a second time in the sauce, & a third time in wine in the stomach."
JOHN RAY, 1670

"On running water, the fly must move in some direction if the trout is to take it."
W. EARL HODGSON, 1907

It is a silly fish that is caught twice with the same bait."
THOMAS FULLER, 1732

"Shredded wheat biscuits may be substituted for clams in Coney Island clam chowder, but not very well."
ROBERTA POLTROON, 1942

"The fishers also shall mourn, & all they that cast angle into the brooks shall lament, & they that spread nets upon the waters shall languish."
ISAIAH XIX, 8 c.700 B.C.

"You're bound to hit bad days on the best of waters."
GRAND TACKLE FONDLER, 1951

"When the wind is in the East
Then the fishies bite the least;
When the wind is in the North,
Then the fishies won't come forth;
When the wind is in the South,
Then the fishies shut their mouth;
But when the wind is from the West
Yellowstone Memorial Garbage Dump,
Wow!"
—Old West Yellowstone Folk Rhyme

"An occasional case of pneumonia is a small price to pay for the pleasure of standing around all day soaking wet in a cold wind, with a fishing rod in your hand."
JOHN BAILEY, 1961

"If you swear you will catch no fish."
ENGLISH PROVERB, c.1607

"The goddam bastids ain't bitin'."
BATWING BEETHOVEN, 1947

Facts about Fish Clubs

Fishermen are notoriously fond of getting together periodically, in order to lie to one another, drink a lot and eat fattening foods. (This is why waders are now manufactured in Extra Large size only.) Annual conventions of the Society of Worm Fishermen, Hello Sucker, Inc., the Militant Mackerel Marchers and others of similar ilk * are occasions of unbridled revelry; fish markets in the area are assured of booming sales at such times.

The photograph (pp. 98–99) was taken during the 1964 conclave of the Federation of Fly Fishermen at West Yellowstone, Montana. Arnold Gingrich, beloved master of ceremonies, is having his toes braided in order to prevent termite infestation and elm blight, while the community's beloved Donna and Millie (kneeling) administer a manicure.

---

* This now-common phrase stems from the earlier West Yellowstone colloquialism, "similar elk." The April, 1927, meeting of the local Elk's club was attended only by Fred and Elmo Riley, who, while not twins, look surprisingly similar. (Other members were too drunk to attend.) Acting secretary Calvin Dunbar was thus inspired to remark, "We've got a lot of similar Elk here today."

"Over yonder," spoke happy Jack, "just beyond the
Girls' Camp, is the part of the lake where the bass
seem to congregate the most! And," added the little
lad, with a merry smile, "often that's where the young
ladies also gather for frolicking and skinnydipping!"

"The only time anyone asks me for a piece of tail,"
sighed Twinky, "is when they want to use it for
hackle in tying up fishing flies."

(CHAPTER XXLIV, "The Sensuous Squirrel")

REVOLUTIONARY NEW

FISHING FACTS

NEVER HERETOFORE UNREELED

Ever wonder why you can't catch fish? "The whole problem lies with your distasteful personality," states an Expert.

So-called angling "authorities" who have gone before (and who should have gone behind) (ha ha) (our Little Joke) have advanced various & sundry theories about success, or lack thereof, in fishing.

Some say the shape and construction of the hook is the mainstay; others maintain the principal secret lies in (a) the rod, (b) the line, (c) the leader, (d) the rubber boots worn by the angler, (e) the fly, lure or worm, (f) time, tide, wind, etc. Let me tell you this right now: all these notions are utter nonsense, as archaic as the belief that rancid chicken fat is harmful to anyone other than chickens.

The true secret of fishing success lies in the personality of the angler. You can have perfectly balanced fishing equipment, good sandwiches, plenty of beer, be able to cast perfectly, etc., and still fail to catch fish. Is this not right? Right! The trouble lies with your personality, which exudes negative ions. And if there is anything that fish detest more than tired, iron-deficient worms, it is negative ions.

HOW FISH DETECT YOUR EXTREMELY UNPLEASANT PERSONALITY

Ichthyologists have scientifically determined that fish can and do detect the revolting smells that your body oils produce and which no amount of

Right Guard, Ice Blue Secret or Mazola can successfully counteract. (Fish hate most products advertised on television, too.)

But your smell problem is only the beginning. In addition, fish don't like fat, blubbery people, and may find you physically unattractive for many other reasons, as well. The sound of your toes squishing in your leaky waders as you walk up the stream is carried for great distances by water currents and is enough in itself to drive fish up the wall. These, together with your negative ions, add up to what I call the FRF, or Fish Revulsion Factor.

DO YOU SUFFER FROM FRF?

If you unknowingly possess the Fish Revulsion Factor it will manifest itself in one of several ways:

1. When you go fishing with other people, they will not only catch more fish than you do, but they will be better sports about it.
2. Waiters will tend to ignore you in restaurants. Most waiters possess amazing telepathic powers and will quickly sense what a rotten person you basically are.
3. Lint tends to gather at the bottom of your pants pockets, caused by your negative ions.
4. Cattle and wild animals that you encounter while out fishing will invariably eye you suspiciously (they sense your negative ions) and look like they are about to charge. Friends may say, "Don't panic; keep your cool." Pay no attention to such bad advice: run like hell.

ARE YOU FRF-FREE?

Maybe you're one of the lucky ones who *doesn't* possess FRF (although chances are against it). Three distinguishing qualities mark such a fortunate fisherman:

1. Love for his fellow man.
2. Generosity toward his fellow man.
3. Concern for his fellow man.

I have devised a simple yet effective little test to determine the presence or absence of these traits, whenever I chance upon some stranger who has succeeded in finding my secret fishing hole, and is angling in same.

Upon detecting the presence of the stranger in my fish paradise, I make it a point to approach him, not by land or in quiet, surreptitious fashion, but by splashing heavily up the middle of the stream itself, often throwing rocks ahead of me to test depths. If the stranger hurries to greet me warmly, shake my hand, etc., he scores on Point 1. I am sorry to report that few indeed have registered a plus point on Love for Fellow Man.

I next engage the stranger in a stimulating conversation (stimulating to me, at any rate) and give him ample opportunity to display his generosity by remarking, "Curse it, sir, but I have just run out of #14 Sparsely Tied Gumfudgin Uprights which I have discovered to be extremely effective in this water, and which I observe you boast a large supply in your hatband." If the stranger then says, "Here, have one of mine," I reply, "Just *one?*"

If he passes the Generosity test, I move on quickly to test his Concern for his Fellow Man with my time-tested remark: "Would you like to have me tell you all about myself?"

HOW CAN YOU OVERCOME FRF?

Assuming (quite safely) that you are possessed of the Fish Revulsion Factor, how can you overcome it? The answer is that *you can't*. There is no known way that you, or anyone like you, can lick this problem. All you can learn to do is face up to this shortcoming, along with all your others. Take up some new hobby where you don't have to come into contact with other intelligent forms of animal life.

Golf, maybe.

"Les Sylphides et les Nightcrawlers"

Artistes from the West Yellowstone Playmill Theatre perform the classic ballet, choreographed by Milford Poltroon, "Les Sylphides et les Nightcrawlers" or "Dance of the Worm Fishermen." Lynn Benson dances the role of the lucky angler who has hooked a 97 lb. brook trout, finned by Jan Telford. Her fish family—(right to left) Robin Squires as Mother Trout, Glen Mahana as Daddy Fish and Byron Sorensen as Uncle Leonard—watch aghast as the fearsome struggle ensues. In the foreground, Angela Williams plays the role of a marshmallow, a favored bait of local fisherfolk.

Performing with her trained carp, "Trigger,"
the lovely Royleena Rogers ("Miss Fort Cus-
ter," 1942) never fails to delight as the star
attraction of the Victory Prune Festival, during
annual Billings Gluttony Days.

Fish of all creeds and colors appear to find both sugar and whiskey enormously attractive.

The as-yet-unsolved problem is how to keep such lures on the hook.

Many anglers have given up the cumbersome and needless practice of carrying a bulky creel, when they go fishing. If, on occasion, the conservation-minded fisherman wishes to bring home a trout or two for a special mealtime treat, he can use a stringer or improvise some other method.

THE JOYS
OF
COMING HOME FISHLESS

Not too many years ago, the angler who returned home fishless was an object of scorn and revilement.

"Yah, yah, yah, here comes old dumbnuts Fred. He didn't ketch no fish today neither."

Today this is all a thing of the past. Conservation groups like the Federation of Fly Fishermen and Trout Unlimited have made "catch-and-release" popular. "Catch-and release" means that after you've had your fun of catching a fish, you let him go, sound and healthy as ever except for a temporary sore lip. In theory, at least, this prevents creeks and puddles from rapidly becoming fish-depleted by ever-growing armies of fisherfolk.

I'm all for it, but for entirely different reasons:

1. It eliminates the need to carry home the enormous fish that I invariably catch, thus relieving both heart and muscle strain.
2. I smell better.
3. It permits me to have hamburger for dinner, which I secretly prefer over fish anyway.

Wearing only hip waders and a Pendleton shirt borrowed from Ralph, and equipped with nothing more than an FF60 2-piece flyrod, lightweight Hardy reel and a double-tapered #5 floating line spliced to a 10-foot knotless leader tapered to an 8X tippet, onto which a #22 Grizzly Wulff with no dressing whatsoever has been tied, the intrepid Jim Green is shot from a large bore cannon, 317 feet above the ground

and over the backs of 3 elephants, as the featured
attraction of Fenwick Brothers, Barnum and Dan
Bailey's Grand Combined Fish Circus. (Regrettably,
2 of the elephants were off sick on the day the
above photograph was taken.) After landing on a
pile of moist Kleenex, Green fearlessly gives demonstrations of how to tie dangerous knots. This inspiring act always "brings down the house."

Early Pioneers Trying to Find West Yellowstone

HOW TO FIND WEST YELLOWSTONE

People continually write to the *Wretched Mess News* to ask, "How can I find West Yellowstone?" The intellectual elite ask, *"Should* I find West Yellowstone?"

The answer to the latter is *exercise caution at all times.* Ever since 1794, when Marianna Chuck dug her first mid-street excavation, the yawning abysses that have been named in honor of the lovely Miss Chuck have been carefully preserved by the community as historical monuments. While Montana Fish & Game has not as yet stocked any of these chuckholes with game fish, they do serve as rest havens for migratory waterfowl, and Jacques Cousteau reportedly plans on exploring some of the deeper ones soon.

A word about the natives of our community may be helpful also. The Yellowstognians, early tribal folk, inhabited West Yellowstone before the coming of the Cleveland Indians and, later, the white man. Noted for their physical development, the men averaged 17 feet tall, but women were much shorter (average 3½ feet). Thus women had to throw rocks at the men to get their attention. This accounts for the abundance of rocks in and about the village, even unto this day. Men were brachycephalic with intelligent faces, unlike present-day descendants. Honest among themselves, they stole from and deceived strangers. Many early tribal customs have remained strong, generation after generation.

Fishing in the area is best the week before you get here and also the day after you depart.

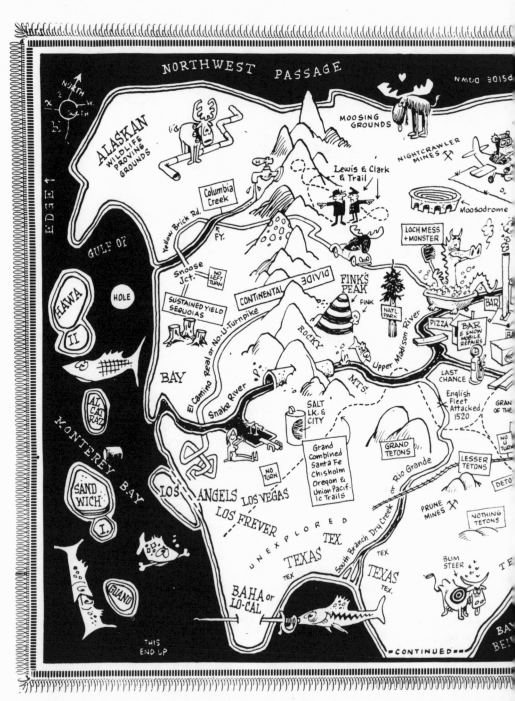

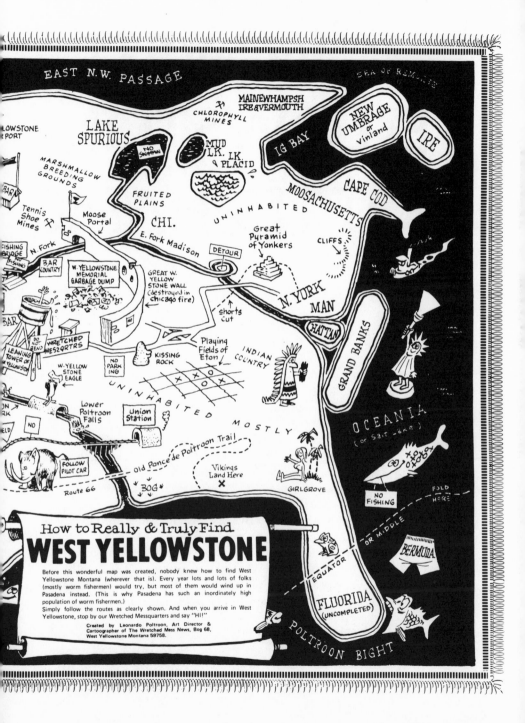

How to Really & Truly Find
WEST YELLOWSTONE

Before this wonderful map was created, nobody knew how to find West Yellowstone Montana (wherever that is). Every year lots and lots of folks (mostly worm fishermen) would try, but most of them would wind up in Pasadena instead. (This is why Pasadena has such an inordinately high population of worm fishermen.)

Simply follow the routes as clearly shown. And when you arrive in West Yellowstone, stop by our Wretched Messquarters and say "HI!"

Created by Leonardo Poltroon, Art Director & Cartographer of The Wretched Mess News, Bog 68, West Yellowstone Montana 59758.

HOW WEST YELLOWSTONE GOT ITS NAME

Traveling west on a 2-seater horse, Clyde and Mortimer Frenzy decided to settle down in the Montana wilderness.

"We'll have to start some sort of business," said Clyde, "in order to make money from passing pioneers."

"Peachy," agreed Mortimer. "So what did you have in mind?"

"A dry cleaning establishment would be nice. People coming out here have to cross the wide Missouri, which is famed for its mud."

"But we don't know anything about dry cleaning," protested Mortimer.

"So who's to know?" asked Clyde.

Thus it was that the brothers started a dry cleaning shop on the very site of what today is Donna Spainhower's snowmobile.

"Suppose somebody comes along who wants something cleaned," said Mortimer, always the worry wart. "What will we use to clean it with?"

"We'll use the things providently provided by a kind Mother Nature," explained Clyde. "Like there's a big nest full of duck eggs in the fetid swamp right behind our establishment. They might serve."

The very next day a notorious gunslinger and 4-string banjo player called "Six-gun Schuler" came by.

"I wish you to clean this utterly lovely pure white vest, of which I am inordinately proud," said Six-gun. "You will note some slight powder burns on the left side which I wish removed."

"Come back for it on Wednesday," said Clyde Frenzy.

The brothers proceeded to clean the vest as best they could with duck eggs from the fetid swamp.

On Wednesday, Six-gun Schuler came by. They handed him his vest. His face grew livid.

"Criminentlies!" he cursed. "You have my *vest yellow stained!*"

A passing Pocatello Indian overheard Six-gun's remark and witnessed his remarkable skill as he shot the livers out of the two brothers. In tribute to Six-gun's fine marksmanship, the Indian thereupon named the place VEST YELLOWSTAINED.

In time, however, the spelling became corrupted together with other things in the area.

"Yes," cried Millie, "I caught four good ones, and all on my little O'Maniac Nymph!"

"I daresay," teased laughing Donna, "that the largest was no bigger than this!"

(CHAPTER XLVII, p. 259, "The Junior League Girls and Their Cookie Drive")

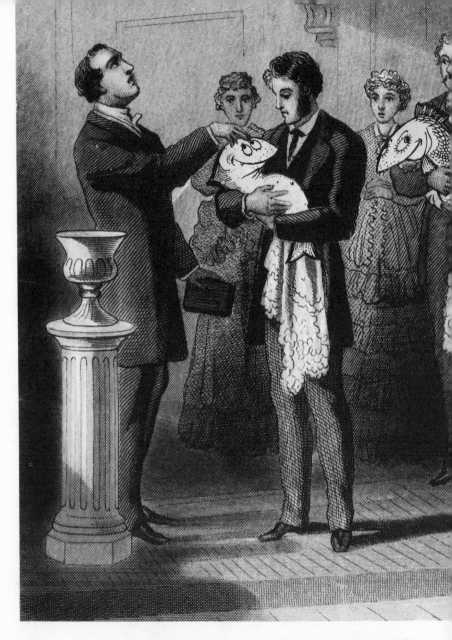

JUDGING FIELD & STREAM'S

In the early days, before fishermen were regarded as entirely trustworthy, anglers who entered *Field & Stream's*
annual contest were required to personally bring their
competing fish to the offices of the publisher, in New
York City, for judging. However, as anglers have since be-

ANNUAL CONTEST

come known internationally for their unwavering veracity, this practice was abolished, and entrants in *Field & Stream's* annual competition now need only to mail in their non-notarized particulars.

LEFTY, GOD OF WORM FISHING

According to ancient Pocatello mythology, Lefty, God of Worm Fishing, was endowed with mystical powers. He was fond of sitting on a large bagel, just outside Blackfoot, Idaho, where he could intercept all northbound anglers. With two of his four arms he offered directions on how to find "West Yellowstone," Montana. Simultaneously, a third arm sold nightcrawlers at prevailing rates, while a fourth arm clutched a bottle of lager beer, from which he frequently quaffed.

Legend has it that Lefty fell in love with Gassina, Goddess of Excess Stomach Acids. One day the two lovers were apprehended while illegally fishing a local creek restricted to flyfishing only. They were using lures constructed from Colorado spinners, Tums and nightcrawlers. This reprehensible act so angered the senior executive gods that they banished the pair forever to downtown Burbank, California.

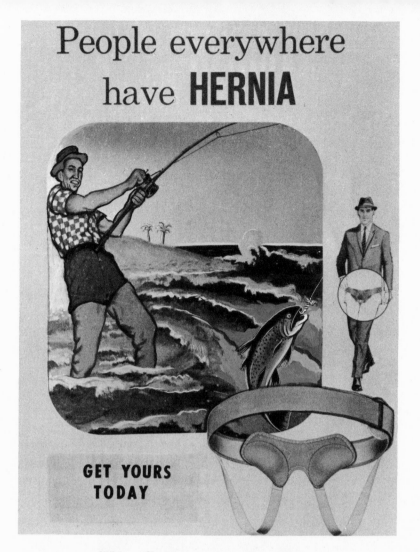

People everywhere have **HERNIA**

GET YOURS TODAY

𝕎𝕙𝕪 𝕀 ℚ𝕦𝕚𝕥 𝕥𝕙𝕖 𝔸𝕕 𝔹𝕚𝕫

I used to be in the ad agency biz until I could no longer abide the blatant dishonesty of ads and commercials that attempt to depict anglers pursuing their sport. The display piece shown above, for a well-known hernia manufacturer, is typical of the misrepresentation that goes on. It shows a fisherman who has hooked into a large rainbow trout in the breakers off Islamorada, Florida (note palm trees in the background), using a heavy surf rod, star drag reel and a large streamer fly. What's wrong, you may ask? Well, no experienced angler in his right mind would dream of fishing in a short-sleeved shirt like the man in the poster wears. The mosquitoes would eat you alive.

121

WORMS ESCAPE FROM LOCAL BAIT & TACKLE SHOP

On June 27, giant nightcrawlers escaped from Jim Danskin's Tackle Emporium in the heart of downtown West Yellowstone, and without apparent provocation, viciously attacked two passing Utah meat fishermen. Proprietor Danskin (right) holds two fingers aloft, to signify that the price of the worms is two bits each, should the tourists wish to purchase them. Shortly after this picture was taken, the visiting fishermen were arrested and jailed for indecent exposure, even though they argued (in vain, as it turned out) that Danskin's worms had eaten their underwear.

Our earliest ancestors were fishermen, as the above ancient petroglyph reveals. Some anthropologists believe there is evidence that present-day fishermen have, in subtle ways, developed beyond their forebears.

"*Yonder lies the fabled Brodheads,*" spoke bright-eyed little Jack, "*as fine a dry fly stream as you'll ever see! But unfortunately,*" he sighed, "*it is privately owned and controlled for most all its length, and unless you belong to some exclusive, high-priced club, they won't let you fish it.*"

"*Now you know,*" replied Twinky, "*what we oppressed minority group members are up against.*"

(CHAPTER CXXVI, p. 832, "Are Red Squirrels Commies?")

A dog has a tail, but the caudal appendage on a rabbit is properly called a 'scut,' while on an otter, it's a 'pole,' on a fox, a 'brush,' on a deer, a 'single,' and on a fisherman, a 'piscatorial posterior,' or 'bass butt.'

A WORD ABOUT

THE AUTHOR

Milford ("Stanley") Poltroon is Editor & Publisher of the *Wretched Mess News*, a piscatorial periodical published out of West Yellowstone, Montana, wherever that is. Many people find it hard to believe that a magazine called the *Wretched Mess News* actually exists; others are equally skeptical about the reality of "West Yellowstone," yet both are genuine and true, even if not altogether sanitary.

Poltroon is, in addition, the creator of the *Wretched Mess Calendar*, which incorporates the first meaningful calendar reforms since acceptance of the Gregorian calendar in 1545. Foremost among Poltroon's calendar improvements is a Genuine Hole for hanging up by, closely followed by nicer paper and the creation of over 399 lovely, unforgettable holidays that no one ever heard of before, and that are completely revised each year. In past years, these have included such joyous occasions as National Fault Finding Week, Questionable Taste Day, Deflour Betty Crocker Day and the anniversary of the day when Ralph Nader replaced St. Christopher.

In an earlier incarnation, Poltroon (under an assumed name) served as Chairman of the Board of a well-known national advertising agency; here he distinguished himself by writing more advertisements and commercials for peanut butter than any other man, living or dead, a record unchallenged even today. But one day in 1966, while recovering in a hospital from a vicious attack by the notorious Dr. Scholl's Footpads, Poltroon reflected that he had allowed peanut butter (especially chunk style) to become more important than fishing, in his life-style. Thus it was that he Heard the Call, Saw the Light and gave up his advertising career to devote his full time to fishing, carousing, increased drinking, publishing the *Wretched Mess News* and other wholesome, worthwhile activities.

ANSWER TO
FISHPUZZLE
BACK THERE ON
PAGE 60

There is no way this puzzle can be
solved according to the rules given.
Those fish weren't as dumb as they
looked, eh?